MOTORCYCLES
A GUIDE TO THE WORLD'S BEST BIKES™

YAMAHA
SPORT RACING LEGEND

rosen publishing's
rosen central

NEW YORK

DIANE BAILEY

Published in 2014 by The Rosen Publishing Group, Inc.
29 East 21st Street, New York, NY 10010

Library of Congress Cataloging-in-Publication Data

Bailey, Diane, 1966–
Yamaha: sport racing legend/Diane Bailey—First edition.
     pages cm.—(Motorcycles: a guide to the world's best bikes)
Includes bibliographical references and index.
ISBN 978-1-4777-1859-9 (library binding)—ISBN 978-1-4777-1878-0 (pbk.)—
ISBN 978-1-4777-1879-7 (6-pack)
1. Yamaha motorcycle—Juvenile literature. I. Title.
TL448.Y3B35 2014
629.227'5—dc23

                                                                                                    2013026210

Manufactured in the United States of America

CPSIA Compliance Information: Batch #W14YA: For further information, contact Rosen Publishing, New York, New York, at 1-800-237-9932.

CONTENTS

INTRODUCTION

Sewing machines or scooters? Auto parts or three-wheeled utility vehicles? Genichi Kawakami faced a decision. The year was 1953, and Kawakami was an executive at a Japanese company that manufactured musical instruments and other products. He was looking for a way to use equipment that had been used to make aircraft propellers. Kawakami chose to expand into the motorcycle market. By 1954, engineers had built their first motorcycle, the YA-1. The "Red Dragonfly" went into large-scale production in 1955, and the Yamaha Motor Company was born.

Immediately, motorcycle racing became an important part of the Yamaha tradition. No sooner had the YA-1 rolled off the production line than Yamaha entered it in two of Japan's premier race events. The bike won in its engine-size class. Over the years, accomplished riders such as Bob Hannah, Kenny Roberts, Chad Reed, and Valentino Rossi have all won on Yamaha bikes—both on pavement and dirt. The "Blue Team" continues to be a competitive force in MotoGP (Motorcycle Grand Prix) racing.

Today, Yamaha is known as the "Tuning Fork" brand because of its presence in the music industry, making musical instruments such as pianos and guitars, as well as accessories. The company is also known for its all-terrain vehicles (ATVs), snowmobiles, and watercraft. In motorcycles, Yamaha has a wide inventory, with sport bikes such as the YZF-R1 and YZF-R6, as well as the YZ-F line of dirt bikes. Another brand, called Star, is owned by Yamaha. Several

touring bikes and cruisers are put out by Star.

Behind Yamaha's reputation for quality and reliability is a concept the company calls "Genesis." With this strategy, Yamaha strives to make all the parts of a motorcycle—from engine to frame to individual parts—work together to make an ideal riding experience. Yamaha calls it "Man-Machine Communication." Its customers just call it "sweet."

Genichi Kawakami *(left)* receives an award from the Belgian government in 1987. Kawakami headed the Yamaha company for most of the years between 1950 and 1983. He died in 2002.

CHAPTER ONE

THE RIGHT FORMULA

Yamaha introduced the YZF-R1 supersport motorcycle in 1998 and has spent the last fifteen years making it better. For proof of that, just ask professional rider Josh Hayes. He took the R1 to three straight championships in the AMA (American Motorcyclist Association) Superbike competition in 2010, 2011, and 2012.

Some help came from Graves Motorsports, a California company that's had a relationship with Yamaha since the R1 first came out. At that time, Graves decided to take the R1 and soup it up to compete in the AMA Formula Xtreme, a series of motorcycle races. With no rules holding them back, the mechanics at Graves were able to develop a line of race parts and accessories for the R1 that transformed it into the ultimate track bike. In the 2002 season, it won every race it entered.

A sport bike must deftly blend top performance on the track with superb street ability. In the highly competitive sport bike market, the YZF-R1 is up against monster machines such as BMW's S1000RR, Honda's CBR1000RR, the Ducati 1199 Panigale, and the GSX-R1000 from Suzuki. The YZF-R1 is a production motorcycle modeled after its MotoGP competitor, the M1. After Valentino Rossi rode to success in the MotoGP World Championship aboard the M1, Yamaha channeled the best racing characteristics of that model into the R1. *Motorcycle USA* said in a review comparing it to similar bikes, "[The Yamaha's engine] makes you feel like you're riding Valentino Rossi's MotoGP bike. Although it's not the fastest, it is by far the most fun and makes the bike easier to ride. Not to mention it's got the coolest feeling."

Several things set the YZF-R1 apart from its rivals. For one, the inline four-cylinder engine gets an extra jolt from a

The YZF-R1 is one of Yamaha's flagship motorcycles. With its own unique feel, this supersport literbike has been ridden to the championship by several professional motorcycle racers.

crossplane crankshaft developed by Yamaha. In addition, the "big bang" engine means that most of the piston strokes happen very close together, which helps enhance traction. Taken together, they give this bike its ferocious performance at the high revs, but with the comforting control and stability of a V-twin.

The 998 cc (61 cubic inches) engine delivers 149 horsepower at 11,900 revs, with 76 lb-ft. of torque, before redlining at 13,600 rpm. However, the bike is a hefty 464 pounds (210 kilograms). That means it sometimes struggles to compete in speed trials on the track, with a

Although it's fine for both street and track, many riders agree the YZF-R1 excels on the road. Its handling delivers a satisfying motorcycling experience and overcomes slightly slower numbers.

top speed of just under 156 mph (251 kph) and acceleration numbers that are on the slower side. A zero-to-sixty run comes in just shy of four seconds. Its weight can also make cornering a tad trickier, and the flick rate—the speed that it can maneuver side-to-side—is slightly slower. Once the bike is set in the corner, though, riders feel a rock-solid stability atop that 55.7-inch (1415 mm) wheelbase.

THE TWO JOSH H'S

Call them the Men in Blue. Dressed in Yamaha's blue and white team colors, professional racers Josh Hayes and Josh Herrin, who are part of Yamaha's racing team, are ready to take on the track. And more often than not, they seem to make their competitors "blue" indeed. Atop Yamaha's YZF-R1, Hayes is a powerful force with the ultimate tool underneath him. His bike bears the number 1—maybe because that seems to be his favorite place in the rankings. In 2012, he notched up his third AMA Pro National Guard Superbike championship in a row. The title was awarded after he claimed a whopping sixteen victories throughout the season.

Hayes's younger teammate, Josh Herrin, started on the YZF-R6, a smaller version of the R1, when he was riding at the Daytona International Speedway but says the R1 is another whole level of bike. It's now one of his favorites. Herrin says, "My favorite thing about the R1 is the sound of that sweet crossplane-crankshaft engine. There's nothing else like it!"

Listen Up

The YZF-R1 has a great sound system, but it has nothing to do with subwoofers. Instead, it's all about the engine. The exhaust note coming out the R1 defines the adrenaline rush that motorcycling is all about. Strictly by the numbers, the R1 doesn't perform as well in highly monitored, racetrack conditions. But the flip side is that motorcycling isn't always about statistics. It's about the feel, and many riders enjoy that the R1 delivers excellent performance at the high revs.

Some friendly competition occurs between Yamaha teammates Josh Hayes *(in front, on number one)*, and Josh Herrin *(number two)*. Hayes won this AMA Superbike race held in 2012 in Alabama.

With the 2012 model, Yamaha introduced a seven-position traction control system, offering six levels of strength, plus a setting where the traction control can be turned off. The system monitors data from sensors that indicate wheel speed and then calculates the difference between the front and rear wheels. If there's too much of a difference, the traction control kicks in. It adjusts the throttle and fuel injection to even things out. The system is extremely sensitive, even more than a rider's instincts, so it can detect problems before the rider. Then it automatically adjusts the settings to create smooth and manageable power. Along with the different traction control settings, the YZF-R1 also offers three different drive modes, increasing or decreasing power for best manageability. Do the multiplication, and that offers twenty-one different engine choices—enough for almost any rider to find a combination that suits his or her style and preferences.

The R1 offers a solid chassis combined with a manageable, if not always magnificent, engine. Most testers agreed it delivered better on the street than the track. It's not the fastest of the superbikes, and it's not the easiest to handle—at least at first. Its size does require skilled handling that isn't always within reach of the average rider. After all, not everyone can be Josh Hayes. But riders noted that even though the Yamaha doesn't muscle up the best numbers, it had a special feel to it that makes it shine as a bike that will probably be ridden more in real-world, not racetrack, conditions.

CHAPTER TWO

THE BACKWARD BIKE

Sometimes, to move forward, you have to take a step backward. Maybe that's what Yamaha was thinking when it redesigned its flagship motocross bike, the YZ450F, for 2010. About the only thing that carried over from the 2009 model was the fact that this was, indeed, still a 449 cc (27 cubic inches) motorcycle. Some people probably wondered why Yamaha would mess with success: the bike had already won the AMA Supercross championship two years in a row, with Chad Reed in the cockpit in 2008 and James Stewart in 2009.

But skeptics soon saw that Yamaha was on to a good thing—a very good thing. *Ultimate Motorcycling* wrote, "Yamaha, with the all-new YZ450F, has fired the first shot in the war to rule the [2010s]. This groundbreaking motocrosser features technical innovations that are highly desirable in the dirt, and may have implications for street bikes in the coming decade."

Unlike other motorcycles in its class, such as Kawasaki's KX450F, Honda's CRF450R, and Suzuki's RMZ450, the new YZ450F switched things around entirely. Most dramatic was the new layout. It reversed the traditional arrangement by offering a rear-slanting engine. This resulted in the air intake being moved

Motocross master James Stewart leads the competition as he goes airborne on Yamaha's YZ450F at the 2009 Monster Energy AMA Super-cross event at the Daytona International Speedway in Florida.

to the front of the bike. There, it cut down on debris coming off the rear tire and allowed designers to create a straighter path of airflow into the engine, heightening performance. In addition, the cylinder was moved to an offset position, creating less friction during combustion. That boosted efficiency. While they were at it, Yamaha's engineers also squeezed a little more out of the compression ratio, or the volume in the combustion cylinder. That resulted in giving the bike more power on the low end.

The bike also got an electronic fuel injection system, with seven sensors that constantly monitor things such as the positions of the throttle and crankshaft, air pressure, and temperature of the air and coolant. It can then automatically adjust the fuel supply to correct imbalances.

Meanwhile, a new chassis design ditched the previous "Y" shape for a double-S. These twin aluminum beams added a little weight but increased the frame's overall strength. They are ideal for dragging in the dirt. The fuel tank is nestled underneath the seat to further concentrate mass toward the center of the bike, which sits on a 58.7-inch (1,491 mm) wheelbase. At 245 pounds (111 kg), the YZ450F is one of the larger and bulkier bikes in its class. However, by tightening the overall layout of the bike and drawing the weight to the center, the YZ450F pulls its mass well around corners.

Handle with Care

When it comes to handling, it takes a little time for riders to get to know the YZ. It is quick, but sometimes a little too

THE FOUR-STROKE REVOLUTION

In the mid-1990s, few people were thinking four-strokes—at least not in the motocross world. The exception was at Yamaha, where engineers were busy building the prototype YZ400M. It was a four-stroker designed specifically for the dirt. Since four-stroke bikes have less power overall, dirt riders had traditionally considered them not good enough to compete with two-strokes. In 1996, the American Motorcyclist Association changed the rules of motocross racing to allow larger displacement four-strokes to compete in the same class as two-strokes with smaller engines. Yamaha engineers designed an engine that drew on superbike technology to make up for the reduced power of a four-stroke. By 1998, the bike had evolved into the YZ400F. That year, rider Doug Henry used it to win the AMA National Motocross Championship. *Cycle World* named it "Bike of the Year." It was a trendsetter that is widely credited with starting the "four-stroke revolution."

quick. Bottom-end power is smooth but not especially ferocious. However, the power builds nicely through the revs, creating steady pull coming into the middle and upper ranges. It doesn't have the mighty top-end strength of some other bikes in this class, but the powerband still offers plenty of verve, and its rock-solid performance there inspires confidence. It has 43.16 ponies snorting at 8,900 rpm, well before the 11,600 rpm redline, and 27.6 lb-ft of torque. A separate power tuner is offered as a handheld device that lets riders change the power characteristics of the engine to fit their preferences.

After many changes for the 2010 model, Yamaha has only tweaked the engine and overall look of the YZ in succeeding years. In 2011, the company improved the clutch, while 2012 brought tinkering to the fuel injection system to make the engine more responsive. Especially at its low and middle ranges, compared to other bikes, the YZ450 has an obedient throttle, offering strong, immediate power at the twist of the wrist. The bike

Competing for Team Yamaha at a Phoenix, Arizona, AMA Supercross event in 2012, motocross rider James Stewart is all smiles. Stewart won several amateur motorcycling titles before turning pro in 2002.

also offers superior suspension, especially in front. Landings out of jumps are stiff enough to fight back while still feeling plush. Footpegs sit higher than those of other bikes in this class, sacrificing a little comfort, but they do make it easier to clear dips in the ground and avoid dragging.

There's no argument that the YZ450F isn't for everyone. Unfortunately for Yamaha, one of those people ended up being star motocrosser James Stewart. In 2012, Stewart, who had been riding the bike for Team Yamaha, jumped ship to Suzuki. He claimed he simply could not adjust to the new YZ450F. However, Stewart later crashed on different bikes, while other riders, such as Chad Reed and Davi Millsaps, both got to the podium on the Yammie. So perhaps it was just a mismatch of man and machine. Even if the YZ doesn't click for every rider, that's not really the point. Its unique styling and features make it different enough from the competition that it's not just more of the same. And for those who can find their groove on it, it really is the only option.

CHAPTER THREE

TAKING THE TOUR

Lose weight! Firm up! Increase energy level!

Perhaps those were Yamaha's New Year's resolutions for the FJR1300A because the 2013 model has done all three. Yamaha's reliable sport touring bike now weighs about 5 pounds (2.3 kg) less than the previous model and offers more shock protection and suspension for a firmer ride. It also boosted its power level by about three horsepower.

Fifteen years ago, when Yamaha engineers were developing the bike, they set a high standard for both the "sport" and the "touring" aspects of the FJR1300A. They required that the bike be stable at a speed of 155 mph (250 kph), while carrying a rider, a passenger, and luggage. The bike was first introduced in Europe in 2001 and came to the United States a year later with the 2003 model. It immediately wowed the critics, pulling in awards as the best touring motorcycle from magazines such as *Cycle World* and *Motorcyclist*. *Cycle World* said, "The FJR combines cruise-ship comfort with a motor that would probably propel an ocean liner at a good clip." The YJR hasn't had a major redesign since it debuted more than a decade ago. However, it has received a collection of minor upgrades that have kept it fresh and competitive.

The big news for 2013 was the addition of the Yamaha Chip Controlled Throttle (YCC-T), borrowed from Yamaha's YZF line of supersport bikes. This "throttle-by-wire" means control of the throttle is handled by the bike's electronics system. That allows the response to be more exact, requiring less effort from the rider. The YCC-T also works in conjunction with other features of the FJR, including traction control, drive modes, and cruise control. As a sport touring motorcycle, it's not surprising that Yamaha has designated its two drive modes as "sport" and "touring." Both can access the full power of the 1,298 cc (79 cubic inches) engine, but in touring mode the power delivery is

Don't get too close: The FJR1300A can show off in a parking lot, but it really excels on the road, where its thirsty 1,298 cc (79 cubic inches) engine combines power with comfort on this sport touring bike.

slightly more muted. It serves up a smoother power curve than the snappier sport mode does. Either way, as riders zoom toward the 9,000 rpm redline, they'll get 144 horsepower at 8,000 revs and 102 lb-ft. of torque. The FJR actually delivers more torque at lower revs—around 4,000 rpm—than competing bikes in this class, making it an easier ride.

The FJR's five-speed transmission is somewhat controversial. Some riders find that the tall upper gear is sufficient at higher speeds and for passing slowpokes on the freeway. Others say a sixth, overdrive gear would be a good addition to the tranny.

TO THE MAX

More is better. That's the rule that Star seemed to follow when it designed the VMAX cruiser. Sure, its muscular styling gives it a look that does everything to reinforce the power cruiser image, but it don't mean nothin' unless it can deliver. No worries. A 1,679 cc (102 cubic inches) engine delivers 160 horsepower and 100 lb-ft. of torque. Put it on a straightaway, and the VMAX roars away from the starting line, making it the ultimate weapon in a drag race. Engineers borrowed technology from Yamaha's YZF series of sport bikes to help the VMAX accelerate to more than 130 miles per hour (209 kph), but raw strength wasn't the only goal for this bike. Even with its long 66.9-inch (1,700 mm) wheelbase and 683-pound (310 kg) weight, handling is surprisingly easy. Some riders are just power hungry. The VMAX has enough to satisfy any appetite.

A Prowling Machine

The fully stressed engine is built into a twin-spar aluminum frame that looks like it could be on a race bike. However, there are enough creature comforts to easily satisfy the pilot for a long-distance ride. On top of the 60.8-inch (1,545 mm) wheelbase, the FJR has a two-position seat, heated hand grips, an adjustable wind screen that lets the rider position it for best airflow, and adjustable air vents to increase or decrease hot air being directed back to the rider. Add in a one-piece, aggressive-looking front fairing and

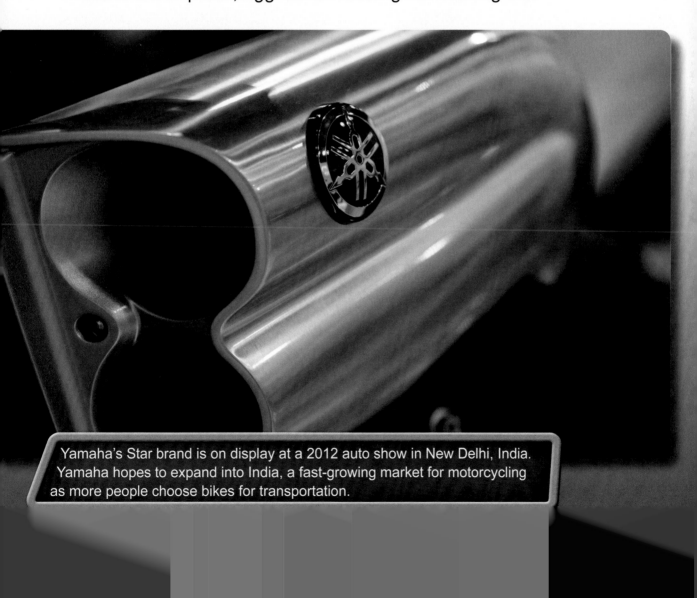

Yamaha's Star brand is on display at a 2012 auto show in New Delhi, India. Yamaha hopes to expand into India, a fast-growing market for motorcycling as more people choose bikes for transportation.

cool LED position lights, and the FJR exudes the attitude of a prowling machine.

Handling is pretty good for such a large bike. Past models of the FJR led some owners to complain that it lacked good control in corners. Improvements to the suspension, which is more stiff overall, help this problem. The FJR has an adjustable front fork and rear shock, with 5.3 inches (13.5 centimeters) of wheel travel in the front and 4.9 inches (12.4 cm) in the back. While it doesn't have the agility to take on the twisties at high speeds, it settles in nicely in more gentle geometry.

The pressure's on when rubber meets the road on the FJR. The tire company Bridgestone noticed this, calling the bike one that "shreds" tires, but Bridgestone answered the challenge by developing tires specifically for the FJR. They give good traction around corners and are designed to provide the durability required by the FJR's 637 pounds (289 kg). Despite the weight of the bike, it has a low center of gravity, which makes it feel lighter and aids in handling.

Up against competitors such as the Triumph Trophy, BMW's K1600, and the Concours 14 from Kawasaki, the FJR1300A delivers. *Cycle News* wrote, "Our first riding impression of the new FJR1300A was a good one and left us wanting more—a lot more. Many things stood out for us but probably none more so than the FJR's just plain good handling....The FJR still feels like an oversized supersport bike, which is a good thing."

CHAPTER FOUR

BEST OF BOTH WORLDS

Street bike? Dirt bike? Survey says...both. When Yamaha introduced the WR250R in 2008, the company was aiming for a specific market segment: people who want it all. In the 250R thumper (a single-cylinder engine), Yamaha designed a bike that blends the characteristics needed for both rugged off-road riding and capable street performance. A day of dirt biking gets more complicated when you have to tow the bike to your destination, so Yamaha set out to make the journey easier—not to mention more fun. This dual-sport is great for beginners or for motorcyclists who are returning to the sport.

An electric starter gets thing moving instantly, setting the 250 cc (15 cubic inches) engine leaping to life. Before hitting the 11,500 rpm redline, it returns about 30 horsepower at 10,000 rpm, and 16.95 lb-ft of torque. Steep hills or higher speeds on the open road mean riders will push the motor on up into its five-digit rpm range, which is where the R really starts to rumble.

A six-speed transmission gives riders control over power that is strong but not overwhelming. The tame bottom end won't be ripping any shoulders out of their sockets, but that just makes it all the easier to get going on the trail. However, the tall gearing may make off-roading more challenging for inexperienced riders.

One feature of the WR250R is the electronic fuel injection, which is a relatively sophisticated feature for this category of bike. That sets it apart from the carburetors of

WR250R

Yamaha has a solid history in the dual-sport category, and one of its current offerings, the WR250R, makes its parents proud, performing well whether it's on the street or in the dirt.

competing bikes such as Honda's CRF230L or Kawasaki's KLX250S.

Maybe the biggest asset to this bike is its suspension. Front and rear suspension settings are adjustable for individual riders to dial in their choices for spring preload and compression and rebound damping. Wheel travel is about 10.6 inches (26.9 cm), and ground clearance is 11.8 inches (30 cm). It's true that the WR250R can't take on the whoops—a series of bumps common to motocross—with the ferocity of a full-on 450 dirt bike. However, it offers pretty decent bump management. A reviewer for *Ultimate Motorcycling* wrote, "[Riding off-road] at high cross-country speeds, I was able to concentrate on my ever-changing lines; the R responded as if it were connected directly to my cerebellum....The R is an excellent way for a street rider to learn about the dirt."

When it introduced the bike in 2008, Yamaha also unveiled another dual-sport, the WR250X. Of the two, the 250R is the more dirt-friendly. That can be seen in the overall styling and design, such as mudguards on the fork. The seat is higher than what is found on a typical street bike, while still low enough not to intimidate newbies. The semi-double-cradle aluminum alloy chassis blends strength and rigidity, and speed is kept under control with disc brakes on the front and rear. Missing are standard handguards or a skid plate under the engine, but those can be added on. The wheelbase measures 55.9 inches (1,420 mm), and overall, the bike feels narrow and compact, with ergonomics designed to absorb the rider into the bike.

DUALIE NOTED

It was 1968, and the times, they were a-changin'. Sure, there were politics and all that. But what mattered to motorcycle buffs was Yamaha's introduction of a bike called the DT-1. Before that machine hit the market, motorcyling was pretty strictly divided between on-road and off-road bikes. The DT-1 took a new approach. Why not do both? It was the perfect "dual-sport" motorcycle, equipped to handle both street and trail riding. No single aspect of the bike was particularly revolutionary, but taken together, they created a bike that no one had seen. Even though it wasn't the first dual-sport, it was the first that was practical and affordable. As such, it's given credit for virtually creating the huge dualie market that continues today. U.S. customers snapped up models as fast as Yamaha could make them. Mitch Boehm of *Moto Retro Illustrated* wrote, "The 1968 DT-1 is more than a contender for Yamaha's most important motorcycle. It's a bike that broke things wide open for the entire Japanese motorcycle industry."

Keep It Legal

When Yamaha was developing the WR250R, the company took some inspiration from its off-road bike, the WR250F. However, the "R" is not simply an "F" with turn signals and a license plate screwed on. Yes, it's got the headlight, taillight, turn signals, and mirrors that make it legal for the street. But

Yamaha introduced this DT-1 250, a dual-sport enduro bike, in 1968. The "Dit One" proved to be an important milestone in motorcycling. It paved—and "dirted"—the way for more dual-sports.

while it shares the overall appearance of the F, that bike is really limited to the dirt, while the R is engineered to work well for street conditions. As a bonus, it has an easier maintenance schedule than most dirt bikes.

Of course, there is some compromise in the equation. The WR250R isn't an enduro bike. At almost 300 pounds (136 kg), it's heavier than a typical dirt bike. On the flip side, even though it can comfortably meet the freeway speed limit—and above—it's not built for serious day-tripping. Instead, it comes down somewhere in the middle.

Although the bike is more expensive than some of its competitors, the price is reflected in the features that make it suited to a wide variety of conditions. It's tough to satisfy two different types of riding with one machine. But as they say: no risk, no reward. Yamaha took the risk, and with the WR250R, riders get the reward.

CHAPTER FIVE

A SUPER ADVENTURE

For years, the competition in the adventure-tourer category was pretty much limited to one bike: BMW's R1200GS. That changed when Yamaha decided it wanted a piece of the action and introduced the Super Ténéré. It matches many of the Beemer's features but brings it all in at a lower price.

Yamaha actually first manufactured the Ténéré back in the 1980s, with the twin-cylinder XTZ750 enduro. That bike racked up six wins in the Paris-Dakar rally, a motorcycle race across Europe and Africa that spanned several hundred miles. The name of the bike comes from the Ténéré region of the Sahara Desert, which was part of the original race.

The revamped Super Ténéré was unveiled in the United States in 2011 with the 2012 model. It is a distinct upgrade from the original '80s version. At its heart is an 1,199 cc (73 cubic inches), parallel-twin cylinder engine. On the way to its 8,000 rpm redline, the engine pumps out 95.1 horsepower at 7,300 rpm, and 75.4 lb-ft of torque. The Super Ténéré plays to the middle with its powerband, lacking a little low-end grunt and top-end scream, but the middle is solid. Also, the delivery is deceptively quiet, so the revs—and speed—climb faster than the rider might expect. Like Yamaha's YZF-R1 sportbike, the Ténéré also has an offset

西ホール
West Hall

SUPER TÉNÉRÉ

In the adventure tourer category, the Super Ténéré competes against other bikes with a smooth powerband delivered from its parallel-twin engine and competent performance both on the road and off.

crossplane crankshaft with an uneven firing order. That lets the bike grab slippery surfaces better, improving traction, while also giving it a distinctive growl.

The Super Ténéré stacks up well against other bikes in its class. It isn't as plush as the BMW, but it does a better job off-roading. Although it lags a bit behind the KTM 990 in the dirt, it offers more overall comfort. In other words, it splits the difference between on-road and off. *Cycle World* said in a review, "One look at the Yamaha Super Ténéré and thoughts of riding to Alaska or South America immediately fill your head, even if all you ever do is cruise to work....If you want to open up more destinations on the map than any other motorcycle, the Super Ténéré is the one to ride."

Out of the Box

Rider comfort comes in the form of a steel chassis with an aluminum subframe for flexibility off-road. The stressed engine takes the place of lower rails that would offer more off-road protection, but there are other ways to make the Ténéré more dirt-worthy. An aluminum skid plate is offered as an extra, as are optional crash bars. The radiator is mounted on the side, pushing the engine forward on the chassis and transferring about half of the bike's total weight to the front wheel.

One cool extra is found in the footpegs, which come with a center rubber insert. For street riding, the rubber offers a nice cushion. When a standing position is needed for off-roading, the rider's weight depresses the rubber, and the

THE DAKAR RALLY

Most people, after they get lost, are just happy to get home. But French motorcyclist Thierry Sabine was ready to do it again—sort of. In 1977, Sabine was riding in a motorcycle rally when he got lost in the Libyan desert. The next year, he organized a rally that would take other riders through the desolate landscape with which he had become enchanted. The rally stretched across Europe and Africa, from Paris, France, to Dakar, Senegal. The endurance race became an annual event and is open to cars and trucks as well as motorcycles. It includes a lot of hostile riding conditions and can be very dangerous. Some competitors have even died during the race. Over the years, the route of the original rally has changed because of political reasons. It has even been held on other continents. But the spirit remains, and Sabine's original motto for the race still holds: "A challenge for those who go. A dream for those who stay behind."

teeth on the rim of the footpeg grab the rider's boot to help keep him or her in place.

The Yamaha is somewhat heavier than other bikes in this class. That's noticeable in turns, although for the most part the bike carries its weight of 578 pounds (262 kg) well, and it has a stable wheelbase of 60.6 inches (1,539 mm). Meanwhile, wheel travel is a comfy 7.5 inches (19 cm) front and back, and the spring preload, compression, and rebound

Thousands of motorcycles compete in an enduro event, Le Touquet, in France. The Super Ténéré, named for a region in Africa where a similar race began, is a popular choice for rallies such as these.

damping are all adjustable. That makes it easier to accommodate a passenger, and with this type of bike, two-up riding comes about as standard as saddlebags.

Two drive modes allow the pilot to control how the engine responds. "Touring" allows for a smoother, less aggressive ride. "Sport" puts a little more power in the hands of the rider. A six-speed transmission finishes with an overdrive gear for freeway cruising.

Stopping power is handled by four-piston calipers on the twin front discs and a single disc on the rear. The Unified Brake System (UBS) lets the rider operate both front and rear brakes simultaneously with the front brake lever, while an additional foot pedal operates just the rear. The Yamaha also comes standard with an antilock brake system, but it has no "off" position. That can be a drawback for serious off-roaders who want the option to lock the rear wheel and spin.

Don't even bother trying to keep up with the electronic control unit (ECU). It's faster than even the most genius math whizzes, measuring wheel speed and other data every one-thousandth of a second. It then transmits the information to the brakes to correct for problems automatically before the rider has to.

When Yamaha was developing the Super Ténéré, the company may have taken notes on BMW's "Boxer" engine, but engineers thought out of the box, too—enough so that the Ténéré is its own creation.

CHAPTER SIX

FAZED IN

They say you can't please everyone.

That's not to say you can't try, and Yamaha did a pretty good job when it introduced the 2011 FZ8. The company calls this bike a blend of "streetfighter attitude and sportbike manners." It's marketed to customers who want it all but don't have room in their garages—or their budgets—to buy multiple motorcycles.

Modeled after the larger, one-liter FZ1 sport bike, the FZ8 brings things down a notch, offering a smaller engine with a 779 cc (48 cubic inches) displacement instead of 1,000 cc (61 cubic inches). At the same time, it offers more power than the smaller FZ6R, which has a 600 cc (37 cubic inches) displacement engine. With the FZ8, Yamaha is playing squarely to the middle. That's not to say the FZ8 is boring. Instead, it's got the nimble qualities of a smaller sport bike, combined with stability and power that make it capable of performing at higher speeds.

The FZ line borrows its engine design from the company's sport bikes, the R1 and R6, but the FZs have been retooled to deliver more mid-range power for better street performance. Start-up is fast and cooperative, and fuel injection makes the throttle smooth across the powerband. Even inexperienced riders who lack skill in the art of throttle-twisting will

MIDDLEWEIGHT MADNESS

Riders must choose a bike that fits their size and style. Manufacturers have to make a bike that fits not only the rider but also the market. Several years ago, Yamaha realized that it had too many bikes serving one type of rider, and not enough serving another. The problem, specifically, came up in the middleweight segment. In the 600 cc (37 cubic inches) class, the company had the Diversion 600 and the XJ6 (a naked version of the Diversion), as well as the FZ6 and 600 Fazer. These four bikes were too similar to each other, and the category was too crowded. Yamaha discovered that it was essentially competing with itself. Meanwhile, it had nothing in the middleweight range. Hmmm. What's halfway between 600 and 1,000?

Yamaha plugged the hole by discontinuing the FZ6 and 600 Fazer, and replacing them with sized-up versions, the FZ8 and Fazer8. At 779 cc (48 cubic inches), these engines offered significantly more power than the 600s but still were a comfortable step down from the monster FZ1. At first offered only in Europe, Yamaha imported the bike to the United States in 2011.

be hard-pressed to stall the engine. *Motorcycle News* noted, "It's a happy rider who cuts through town traffic like a needle through tissue and the FZ8 is a good tool for such use."

Making the Switch

To make the FZ8, Yamaha engineers first borrowed the inline, four-cylinder engine from their YZF-R1 sport bike. Next they narrowed the bore to shrink the displacement and shaved off some weight. Then they redesigned the camshafts, with the effect of squishing the power curve, allowing more power down low while keeping the middle manageable. The result is that the FZ8 offers more power and torque at low and mid-range rpm. However, the engine is happier once it gets going, above 4,000 revs. It snorts out 95.7 horsepower at 10,000 rpm, before the rev limiter tops

The middleweight FZ8 offers an option to riders who want a little more power in the cockpit than a 600 cc (37 cubic inches) bike gives, but who still demand nimble handling for navigating tight turns or tough traffic.

out at 11,500, and delivers 61 lb-ft. of torque. That's significantly more than a 600 cc (37 cubic inches) engine, but the FZ8 still offers about the same amount of agility as a smaller bike.

The gearbox, while similar to the FZ1's, has been tuned to work with the FZ8's smaller size, with a shorter first gear that quickens the overall pace of the acceleration and gets things going more quickly. At the same time, the first gear doesn't sacrifice speed, taking the bike to more than 70 mph (113 kph) before shifting is needed.

One weakness on earlier models of the bike was the lack of adjustable suspension. Except for the preload on the rear, riders were stuck with the factory settings unless they

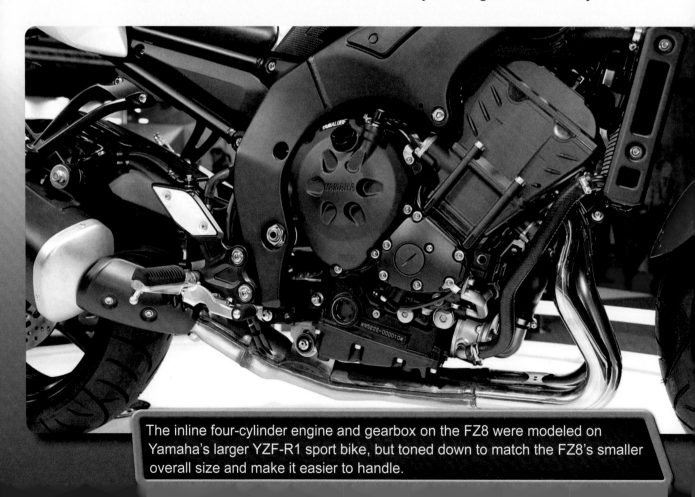

The inline four-cylinder engine and gearbox on the FZ8 were modeled on Yamaha's larger YZF-R1 sport bike, but toned down to match the FZ8's smaller overall size and make it easier to handle.

went to aftermarket products to tinker with the numbers. For the 2013 model, Yamaha made things easier. The front fork now allows adjustable rebound and compression damping, while the rear shock offers adjustable preload and rebound damping. Both front and back offer 5.1 inches (13 cm) of wheel travel.

At 467 pounds (212 kg), the FZ8 is lighter than its big brother, but it's still on the heavy side for others in its class, such as the 675 cc (41 cubic inches) Triumph Street Triple or the 798 cc (49 cubic inches) BMW F800R. However, a low center of gravity helps disguise its mass, and once underway, the 57.5-inch (1,461 mm) wheelbase isn't grunting under the weight. Also, the FZ8 has no front fairing or windscreen, which reduces the weight a little more. That does come with a cost because the lack of wind protection means long rides can subject the rider to buffeting. On shorter hauls though, say, 100 miles (161 km) or so, it's a relatively comfortable ride. The riding position is largely standard, but it is slightly more aggressive than on the FZ1, with the footpegs set a smidge lower and farther back, and the handlebars a tad more forward. That brings the rider down a little bit and helps make up for the lack of a windscreen.

Overall, the FZ8 offers good power and strength but tones it down just enough to match its more compact measurements. When the FZ8 hit the U.S. market, *Motorcycle Daily* said, "The bike has a completely different character than an FZ1 and, in many ways is both superior and cheaper to own."

SPECIFICATION CHART

YZF-R1

redline	13,600 rpm
horsepower	149 @ 11,900 rpm
torque	76 lb-ft.
transmission	6 speeds
fuel capacity	4.8 gallons / 18.2 liters

YZ450F

redline	11,600 rpm
horsepower	43 hp at 8,900 rpm
torque	27.6 lb-ft.
transmission	5 speeds
fuel capacity	1.6 gallons / 6.1 liters

FJR1300A

redline	9,000 rpm
horsepower	144 at 8,000 rpm
torque	102 lb-ft.
transmission	5 speeds
fuel capacity	6.6 gallons / 25 liters

WR250R

redline	11,500 rpm
horsepower	30 hp at 10,000 rpm
torque	16.95 lb-ft.
transmission	6 speeds
fuel capacity	2.0 gallons / 7.6 liters

SUPER TÉNÉRÉ

redline	8,000 rpm
horsepower	95.1 hp at 7,300 rpm
torque	75.4 lb-ft.
transmission	6 speeds
fuel capacity	6.0 gallons / 22.7 liters

FZ8

redline	11,500 rpm
horsepower	95.7 hp at 10,000 rpm
torque	61 lb-ft.
transmission	6 speeds
fuel capacity	4.5 gallons / 17.0 liters

GLOSSARY

ALLOY A metal made by combining two or more different metals.

CROSSPLANE CRANKSHAFT The part of the engine that converts piston motion into rotation, using pins arranged at 90-degree angles to each other.

DAMPING The process of controlling how much suspension a bike delivers.

DUAL-SPORT A type of motorcycle that can be used both on- and off-road.

ENDURO A type of motorcycle designed for off-road riding.

ERGONOMICS Materials and designs used to improve physical comfort.

EXHAUST NOTE The distinctive sound a motorcycle makes.

FAIRING A covering on the front portion of a motorcycle offering wind protection.

FORK Metal tubes that connect the front wheel to the motorcycle frame.

MOTOCROSS A type of motorcycle racing held on closed circuits with rough terrain.

POWERBAND The range of rpm in which a bike performs most effectively.

PRODUCTION MOTORCYCLE A motorcycle that is available to the general public and has not been modified from its original form.

PROTOTYPE The first example or model of something.

REDLINE The highest limit of the engine's revolutions per minute (rpm).

STRESSED ENGINE An engine that is an integral part of the motorcycle's overall physical design.

SUPERBIKE A sport bike with an engine displacement of 1,000 cc (61 cubic inches) or more.

TORQUE The tendency of a force to produce a rotation.

FOR MORE INFORMATION

American Motorcyclist Association (AMA)
13515 Yarmouth Drive
Pickerington, OH 43147
(800) 262-5646
Web site: http://www.americanmotorcyclist.com
Founded in 1924, the AMA is the world's largest motorcycling
organization.

Motorcycle Safety Foundation (MSF)
2 Jenner, Suite 150
Irvine, CA 92618
(800) 446-9227
Web site: http://online2.msf-usa.org/msf
The MSF offers courses in safe, responsible motorcycle
operation, and advocates for safer riding conditions.

Motorcycle Sport Touring Association (MSTA)
P.O. Box 2187
Manchaca, TX 78652
Web site: http://www.ridemsta.com
The MSTA organizes events for sport touring motorcylists
and unites enthusiasts of this branch of motorcycling.

National Motosport Association (NMA)
P.O. Box 891299
Temecula, CA 92589
(951) 587-9805
Web site: http://www.nmamx.com

The NMA, founded in 1970, sponsors the World Mini Grand Prix, an annual motocross competition for young riders.

Women on Wheels (WOW)
P.O. Box 83076
Lincoln, NE 68501
(402) 477-1280
Web site: http://www.womenonwheels.org
Founded in 1982, WOW serves as an organization to bring together women interested in motorcycling.

Yamaha Motor Corporation, USA
6555 Katella Avenue
Cypress, CA 90630
(800) 962-7926
Web site: http://www.yamaha-motor.com
Yamaha's American headquarters has information on the company's product line and provides assistance to Yamaha customers.

Web Sites

Due to the changing nature of Internet links, Rosen Publishing has developed an online list of Web sites related to the subject of this book. This site is updated regularly. Please use this link to access the list:

http://www.rosenlinks.com/MOTO/Yama

FOR FURTHER READING

Adamson, Thomas K. *Freestyle Motocross* (Blazers: Dirt Bike World). North Mankato, MN: Capstone Press, 2010.

Adamson, Thomas K. *Motocross Racing* (Blazers: Dirt Bike World). North Mankato, MN: Capstone Press, 2010.

Ames, Michael, and Jonny Fuego. *Cruisers*. Layton, UT: Gibbs Smith, 2009

David, Jack. *Enduro Motorcycles*. Minneapolis, MN: Bellwether Media, 2008.

Doeden, Matt. *Enduro Racing* (Blazers: Dirt Bike World). North Mankato, MN: Capstone Press, 2010.

Gillespie, Lisa Jane. *Motorcycles*. London, England: Usborne Books, 2011.

Henshaw, Peter. *The Encyclopedia of Motorcycles, Vol. 5: Suzuki-ZZR.* New York, NY: Chelsea House Publishers, 2000.

Holter, James. *Dirt Bike Racers* (Kid Racers). Berkeley Heights, NJ: Enslow Publishers, 2010.

Mason, Paul. *Dirt Biking; The World's Most Remarkable Dirt Bike Rides and Techniques.* North Mankato, MN: Capstone Press, 2011.

Oxlade, Chris. *Motorcycles* (How Things Work). Collingwood, Ontario, Canada: Saunders Book Company, 2011.

Stealey, Bryan. *Motocross* (Racing Mania). Tarrytown, NY: Marshall Cavendish, 2009.

Streissguth, Thomas. *Standard Motorcycles*. Minneapolis, MN: Bellwether Media, 2008.

West, Phil. *Superbikes: Machines of Dreams* (Gearhead Mania). New York, NY: Rosen Classroom, 2012.

BIBLIOGRAPHY

Ash, Kevin. "Yamaha Super Ténéré Test." AshonBikes.com. Retrieved January 6, 2013 (http://www.ashonbikes.com/content/yamaha-super-t%C3%A9n%C3%A9r%C3%A9-test).

Dean, Paul. "2013 Yamaha FJR1300A—Riding Impression." *Cycle World*, November 30, 2012. Retrieved December 27, 2012 (http://www.cycleworld.com/2012/11/30/2013-yamaha-fjr1300a-riding-impression).

Garcia, Frankie. "2013 Yamaha FZ8 First Look." *Motorcycle USA*, October 2, 2012. Retrieved January 6, 2013 (http://www.motorcycle-usa.com/649/14446/Motorcycle-Article/2013-Yamaha-FZ8-First-Look.aspx).

Waheed, Adam. "2012 Yamaha YZ450F Comparison." *Motorcycle USA*, January 4, 2012. Retrieved January 2, 2013 (http://www.motorcycle-usa.com/276/11853/Motorcycle-Article/2012-Yamaha-YZ450F-Comparison.aspx).

Waheed, Adam. "2012 Yamaha YZF-R1 Track Comparison." *Motorcycle USA*, June 25, 2012. Retrieved January 2, 2013 (http://www.motorcycle-usa.com/268/13483/Motorcycle-Article/2012-Yamaha-YZF-R1-Track-Comparison.aspx).

Williams, Don. "2008 Yamaha WR250R and WR250X—Motorcycle Test." *Ultimate Motorcycling*, June 1, 2008. Retrieved January 4, 2013 (http://ultimatemotorcycling.com/2008_yamaha_wr250r_wr250x).

INDEX

About the Author

Diane Bailey has written more than thirty nonfiction books for teens, on subjects ranging from sports to states to celebrities. She has two sons and two dogs, and lives in Kansas.

Photo Credits

Designer: Brian Garvey; Editor: Bethany Bryan;
Photo Researcher: Karen Huang